PUMPKIN CARVING STENCILS

50 HALLOWEEN TEMPLATES FOR CARVING PUMPKINS, DECORATING AND PAINTING CRAFTS

HOW TO USE

Wipe down pumpkin, make sure it's clear of dust and dirt.
Cut the top or bottom of your pumpkin inwards at an angle of 45 degrees.
This will make sure your lid will not fall into your pumpkin.

Remove the pulp and seeds of the pumpkin with a scoop or spoon.
Scrape the inside until the pumpkin wall is about 1" (2.5 cm) thick.

Select your preferred design.
Cut the page out and tape the stencil to the flattest side of your pumpkin.
NOTE: You may need to cut slits around the stencil so that it will lay
smoothly and fit the curve of your pumpkin.

Trace the design onto the pumpkin by poking holes along the edges of the black areas.
To make the holes, use the tip of a sharp pencil, needle, or poker tool.
Make sure the holes are closely spaced.
Before removing stencil, double-check that all the design details were traced.

Use a pumpkin carving saw, or serrated craft knife to cut along the traced holes.
Use the stencil or the preview image on the stencil pages (bottom right)
as a reference for where to carve out the design.
The black area of the stencil is what will be carved out.

TIP: start carving from inside the design and work your way outward

Place a candle, or battery powered light inside the pumpkin and enjoy!

QUICK TIPS

Choose a pumpkin that will give you enough surface to carve out your design.

Select a pumpkin with a consistent orange color, that sits flat on the ground;
make sure it's free of bruises and soft spots.

✷ BLACK AREA IS THE CARVE OUT AREA ✷

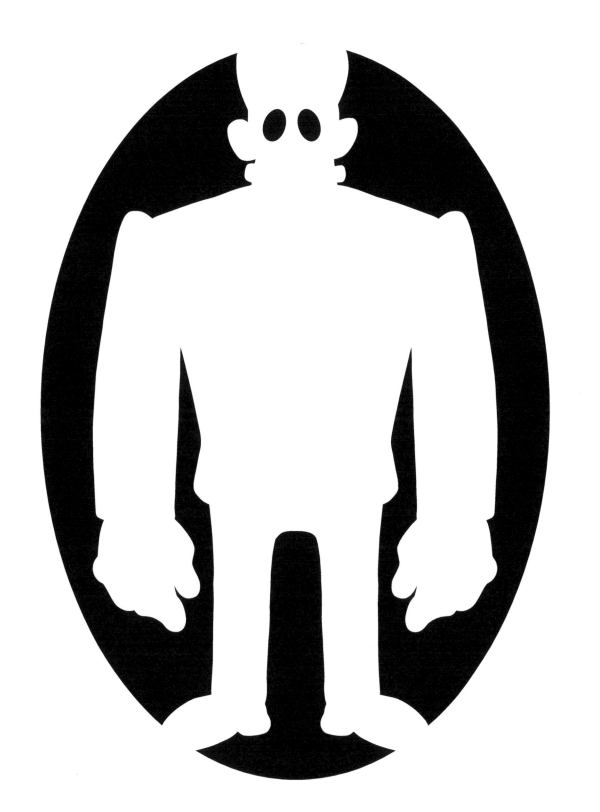

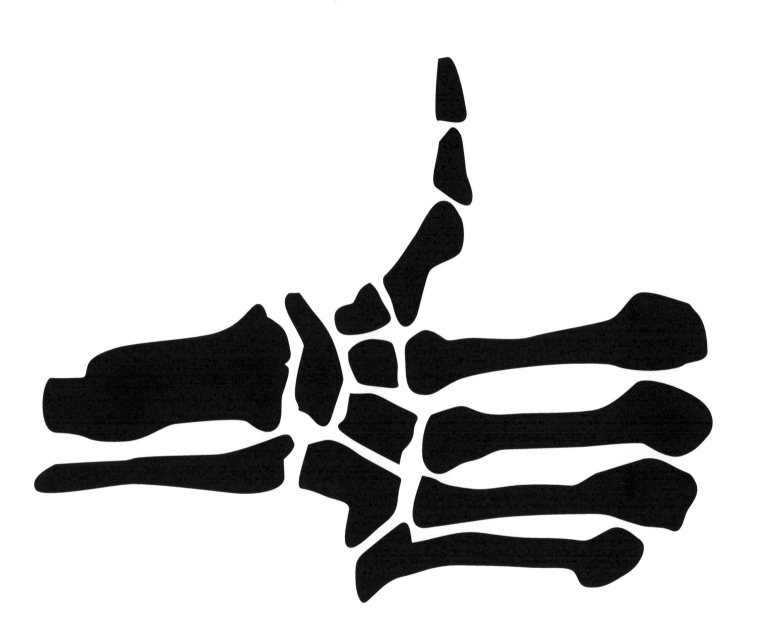

SPOOKY

Printed in Great Britain
by Amazon